How cute is this **LIFESIZE** baby otter? Most baby sea otters are born in the water but they prefer to lie on their mummies' tummies and bob about together on the sea. AWWWWWW!

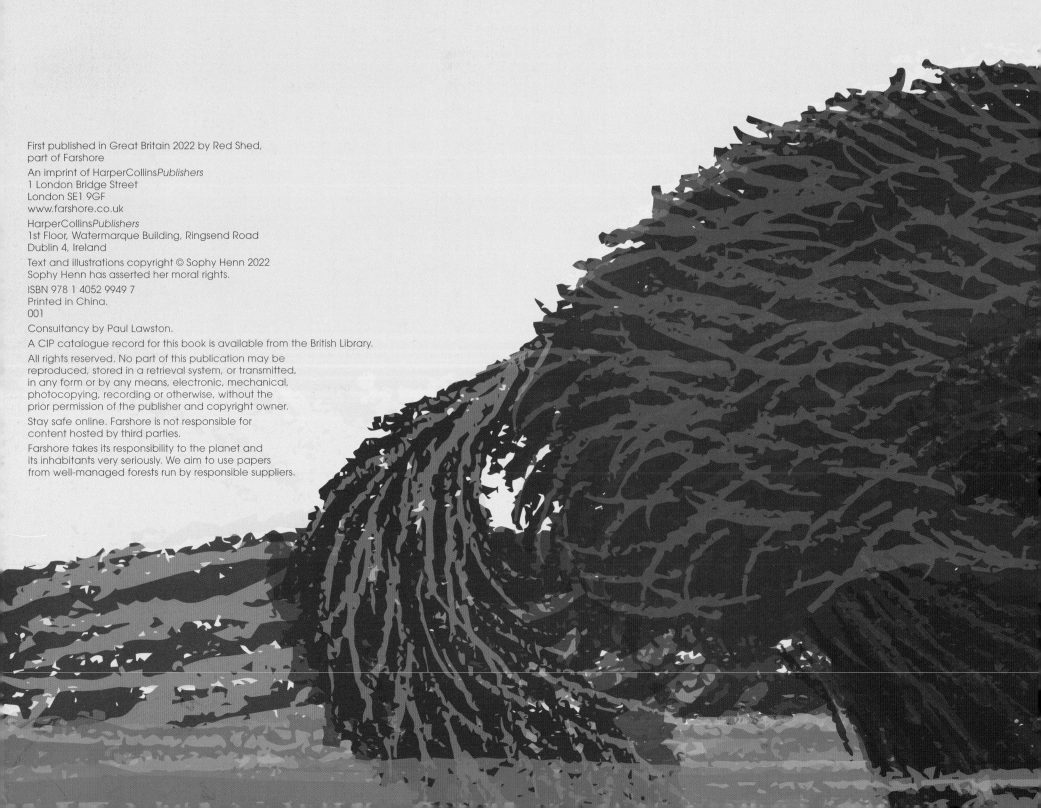

First published in Great Britain 2022 by Red Shed,
part of Farshore

An imprint of HarperCollins*Publishers*
1 London Bridge Street
London SE1 9GF
www.farshore.co.uk

HarperCollins*Publishers*
1st Floor, Watermarque Building, Ringsend Road
Dublin 4, Ireland

Text and illustrations copyright © Sophy Henn 2022
Sophy Henn has asserted her moral rights.

ISBN 978 1 4052 9949 7
Printed in China.
001
Consultancy by Paul Lawston.

A CIP catalogue record for this book is available from the British Library.

LIFESIZE

Sophy Henn

BABY ANIMALS

RED
SHED

The world is full of lots of amazing animals. So it makes perfect sense that it is full of lots of amazing BABY animals too – from the super small to the absolutely MASSIVE! But just how super small and absolutely massive are they?

Well, you can see for yourself because every time you see the word LIFESIZE in this book, you will know you are looking at an animal, or a bit of an animal, that is the actual size it is IN REAL LIFE!

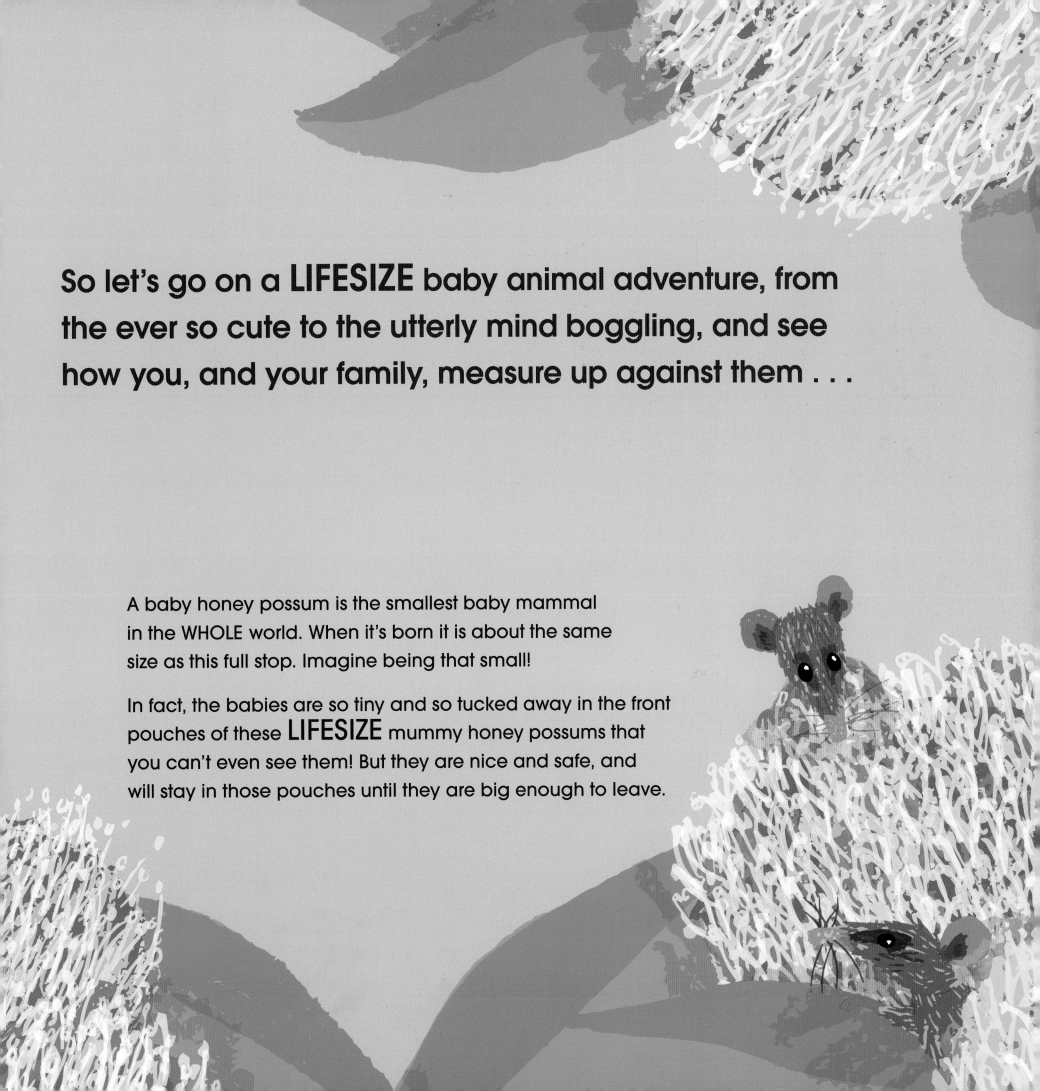

So let's go on a **LIFESIZE** baby animal adventure, from the ever so cute to the utterly mind boggling, and see how you, and your family, measure up against them . . .

A baby honey possum is the smallest baby mammal in the WHOLE world. When it's born it is about the same size as this full stop. Imagine being that small!

In fact, the babies are so tiny and so tucked away in the front pouches of these **LIFESIZE** mummy honey possums that you can't even see them! But they are nice and safe, and will stay in those pouches until they are big enough to leave.

WOW! You are looking into the eye of a **LIFESIZE** baby blue whale, the biggest baby in the world! When they are born, blue whales are already the same size as an ambulance and they grow up to be as long as two buses!

Here is a **LIFESIZE** baby flamingo. No, really! You see, flamingoes are born grey and slowly turn pink from all the algae and shrimps they eat. What colour would you be if you turned the same colour as your favourite food?

These **flamingoes** live in the hot, leafy mangrove forests of Mexico. They eat with their heads upside down, using their beaks to filter out their food.

Who else lives here?

Look at these LIFESIZE baby nine-banded armadillos! They are always born in sets of four identical pups.

Spider monkeys have one baby at a time, and that baby clings to its mummy's tummy as she moves about. They got their name because when they hang from trees by their super strong tail they look like spiders!

Tapirs have one baby at a time too, and they are born with markings that help camouflage them from predators. They also look pretty snazzy!

WOW! Look at all of these LIFESIZE
baby zebra seahorses – they are
so tiny and there are so many of them.

It's actually seahorse daddies that give birth:
to up to **2,000 AT ONE TIME!** Can you imagine
having that many brothers and sisters . . .
How would you remember all their names?

Zebra seahorses live on the beautiful coral reefs of Australia alongside these other amazing creatures . . .

Before these tiny **LIFESIZE** baby blue-ringed octopuses hatched, their eggs were kept safe and warm under their mother's arms.

These **LIFESIZE** baby rays started life as eggs, which hatched INSIDE their mum and before they were born.

These **LIFESIZE** baby green turtles hatched out of eggs buried in the sand on the beach. Handily they were born with a special 'egg tooth' to help them break out of their egg.

This **LIFESIZE** baby black bear is super cute, and it's also growing super fast. In fact, in their first three months baby black bears grow to be more than three times as big as they were when they were born.

How big would you be in three months' time if you grew that fast?

Black bears are mainly found in the mountain forests of North America, along with these other animals . . .

Wolf pups are born with blue eyes that gradually turn yellowish gold before they reach four months old. When the pups are fully-grown, their sense of smell will be 100 times stronger than ours.

How cheeky do these **LIFESIZE** raccoon kits look? VERY! But when their mum needs to go somewhere, the kits will all line up behind her and follow in an orderly fashion!

Look! A **LIFESIZE** red panda nest,
with a mummy and her cubs . . . COSY!

To keep extra-warm, the red pandas wrap their tails, which are three-quarters as long as they are, around themselves. Imagine having a tail almost as tall as you, that you could wear like a scarf!

Red pandas live in the sometimes snowy hills of China, BRRRRRR! They make their nests high up in tree branches or in holes in tree trunks.

But who are their neighbours?

Well, there's the clouded leopard
These cubs will grow into exper
climbers, able to hang upside down
from tree branches

Here is a **LIFESIZE** baby golden snub-nosed monkey with its mummy. When it gets really cold at night, groups of mummies and babies all snuggle up together in 'sleep clusters' to keep warm.

Here is a LIFESIZE baby African elephant.

It's really tall for a baby, isn't it?

Is it as tall as you are now?

And its ears are the same size as its face!

I bet your baby pictures would have looked

very different if you had been born with ears

as big as YOUR face . . . .

Elephants use their trunks to drink water and they can hold up to 8 litres! GULP! African elephants live in Africa – well of course they do!

But who else lives there?

Baby giraffes fall almost 1.5 metres to the ground when they are born, arriving into the world with a BUMP!

Look at these teeny tiny LIFESIZE baby African leaf chameleons! They can change colour just as soon as they are born and use this skill to communicate with other chameleons.

Baby cheetahs are born with a furry mohawk all down their back (it's actually called a mantle) and this helps them to camouflage in the long grass.

Warthogs live in burrows that they have stolen from aardvarks. **Naughty!** The mummies let their piglets go into the burrow first and then back in after them so they can protect them from predators.

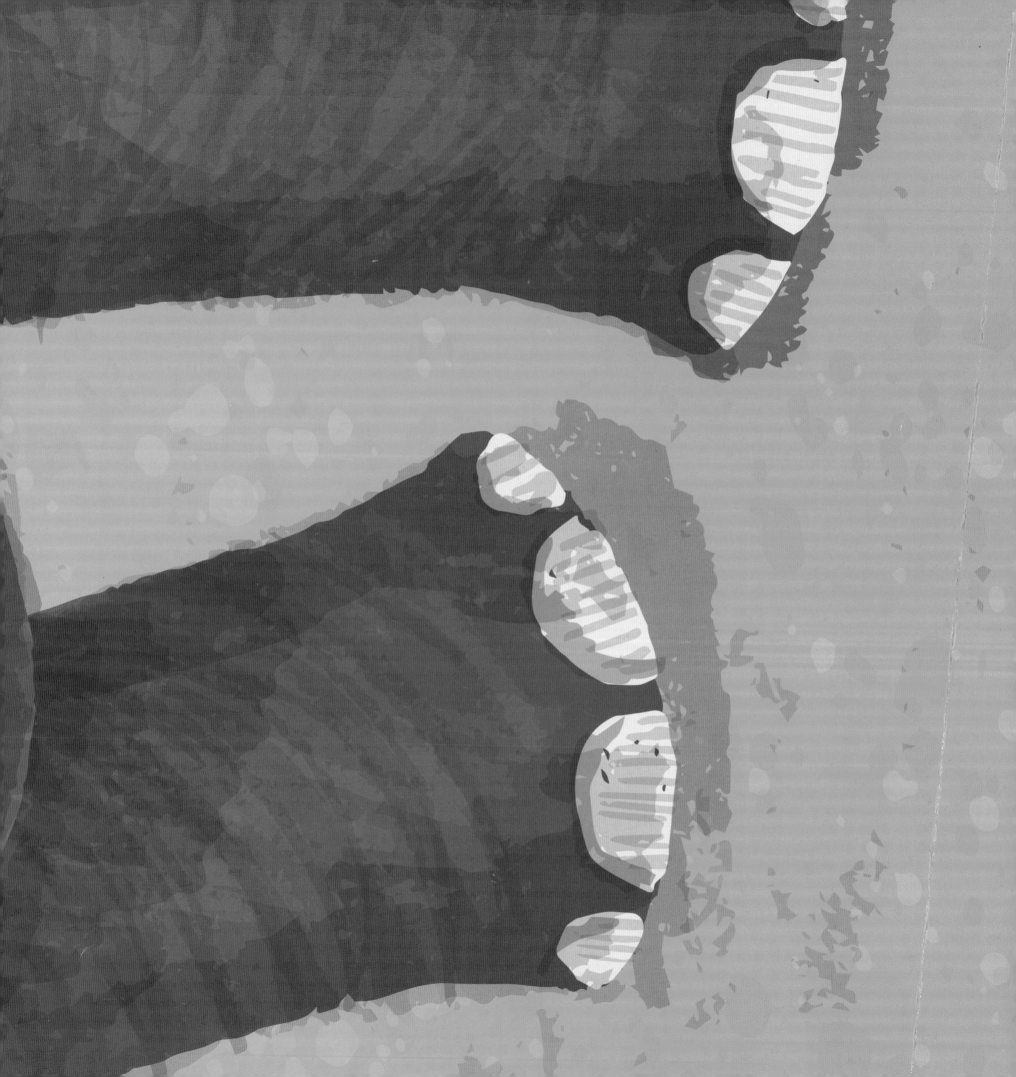

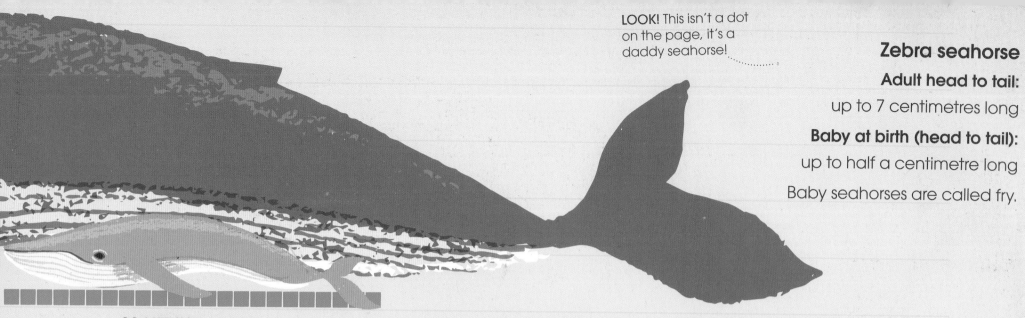

LOOK! This isn't a dot on the page, it's a daddy seahorse!

Zebra seahorse

Adult head to tail:

up to 7 centimetres long

Baby at birth (head to tail):

up to half a centimetre long

Baby seahorses are called fry.

23 LIFESIZE books

100 LIFESIZE books

Can you work out where you fit into the line-up? Measure yourself using this book and see how you compare. Maybe you could measure some of your family and see how they compare too!

Sea otter

Adult (head to tail):

up to 1.2 metres long

Baby at birth (head to tail):

up to 60 centimetres long

Baby otters are called pups or kittens.

2 LIFESIZE books

4 LIFESIZE books

Honey possum

Adult (head to tail):

up to 9 centimetres long

Baby at birth (head to tail):

up to half a centimetre long

Baby possums are called joeys.

American black bear

Adult (head to tail):

up to 1.8 metres long

Baby at birth (head to toe):

up to 20 centimetres long

Baby bears are called cubs.

Red panda

Adult (head to tail):

up to 1.2 metres long

Baby at birth (head to tail):

up to 20 centimetres long

Baby pandas are called cubs.

of a LIFESIZE book

6 LIFESIZE books

4 LIFESIZE books

$\frac{2}{3}$ of a LIFESIZE book

Blue whale

Adult (head to tail):

up to 30 metres

Baby at birth (head to tail):

around 7 metres

Baby whales are called calves.

Wow! We've been all over the world and we have seen some incredible **LIFESIZE** baby animals.

Let's see how they compare as babies,

and when they are all grown up!

1 LIFESIZE book

5 LIFESIZE books

Orang-utan

Adult (head to toe):

up to 1.5 metres

Baby at birth (head to toe):

up to 30 centimetres

Baby orang-utans are called babies.

African elephant

Adult (head to toe): up to 4 metres

Baby at birth (head to toe): up to 1 metre

Baby elephants are called calves.

13 LIFESIZE books

3 LIFESIZE books

American flamingo

Adult (head to toe):

up to 1.2 metres

Baby at birth (head to toe):

up to 20 centimetres

Baby flamingoes are called flaminglets.

4 LIFESIZE books

²⁄₃ of a LIFESIZE book